**PRIVATE**

**Colemanballs**

Illustrated by Larry

A selection of quotes
that originally appeared in
PRIVATE EYE's 'Colemanballs'
column.
Our thanks are due to
those sharp-eared readers
who sent us their
contributions.

If you enjoyed this book,
the following best-selling titles
are also available

**Colemanballs 2**
**Colemanballs 3**
**Colemanballs 4**
**Colemanballs 5**

# PRIVATE EYE'S

## Colemanballs

### Illustrated by Larry

Compiled and edited by
**Barry Fantoni**

PRIVATE EYE · CORGI

Published in Great Britain 1982
by Private Eye Productions Ltd,
6 Carlisle Street, London W1V 5RG,
in association with Corgi Books

Reprinted 1982 (five times), 1983, 1984,
1985 (twice), 1986, 1987, 1989, 1991, 1992 and 1993

© Pressdram Limited

ISBN 0 552 13783 9

Printed in Great Britain by
Cox & Wyman Ltd, Reading

Corgi Books are published by Transworld Publishers Ltd,
61–63 Uxbridge Road, Ealing, London W5 5SA,
in Australia by Transworld Publishers (Australia) Pty, Ltd,
15–25 Helles Avenue, Moorebank, NSW 2170
and in New Zealand by Transworld Publishers (N.Z.) Ltd,
3 William Pickering Drive, Albany, Auckland

# Athletics

. . . Marie Scott, from Fleetwood, the 17-year-old who has really plummeted to the top. . .

ALAN WEEKS

She's dragged the javelin back into the
twentieth century.

RON PICKERING

Her time about 4.13, which she's capable of.

DAVID COLEMAN

She never knows when she's beaten except
when she actually is.

STEPHEN HADLEY

. . . as they come through absolutely together
with Wells in first place. . .

DAVID COLEMAN

Two little jumps there — one big one and one
small one.

DAVID VINE

There is Brendan Foster, by himself, with
twenty thousand people. . .

DAVID COLEMAN

He is even smaller in real life than he is on the track.

DAVID COLEMAN

And he can't afford to be beaten because, if he is, he'll be beaten. . .

TONY GUBBA

. . . a very powerful set of lungs, very much hidden by that chest of his.

ALAN PASCOE

Virren, the champion, came in fifth place, and ran a champion's race.

ANON

Within a few hours, in Moscow, the Olympic Flame will have been put into cold storage for another four years.

GORDON CLOUGH

The big guns haven't pulled all the stops out yet.

DAVID COLEMAN

Michelle Ford. . . is Australia's first Olympic
medal for four years.

NORMAN MAY


And our next race is the next race. . .
DAVID COLEMAN


The record is 38 seconds; one of the best times
ever.

DAVID VINE


He is going up and down like a metronome.
RON PICKERING


This man could be a black horse.
DAVID COLEMAN


He won the bronze medal in the 1976
Olympics, so he's used to being out in front.
DAVID COLEMAN


. . . and the crowd are absolutely standing up.
ALAN WEEKS

This boy swims like a greyhound. . .

ATHOLE STILL

. . . he just can't believe what's not
happening to him.

DAVID COLEMAN

Tahamata went through the air like a
torpedo.

PETER JONES

Lillian's great strength is her strength.

DAVID COLEMAN

The loss of a life is — well — the loss of a life,
and that's something you can't take away.

*Secretary*, BRITISH WINTER OLYMPIC TEAM

Both these players seem to anticipate the play
of the other almost before it's happened.

TONY GUBBA

The French are not normally a Nordic skiing
nation.

RON PICKERING

Here we are in the Holy Land of Israel — a
Mecca for tourists.

DAVID VINE

There'll only be one winner now — in every
sense.

DAVID COLEMAN

And the race is all about first, second and third.

HAMILTON BLAND

Harvey Glance, the black American sprinter with the white top and the black bottom. . .

RON PICKERING

There is only one winner in this race.

DAVID COLEMAN

. . . and the winner is the winner.

DAVID COLEMAN

Not so much a false start as a faulty start.
DAVID COLEMAN

Bradford, who had gone up from 200 metres to 400, found it hard going and for the last 100 was always going backwards.
DAVID COLEMAN

Coe has made absolutely no move at all down the back straight.
DAVID COLEMAN

And Brian Hooper will have that recurring dream again and again. . .
RON PICKERING

Henry Rono. . . the man with those tremendous asbestos lungs.

RON PICKERING

# Bowls

DAVID VINE: What's he going to do with this,
do you think?
DAVID RHYS-JONES: Well, he's got to be
thinking that he's got to do something with this.

# Boxing

I was ranked fourth in the world and you know what that means? I was fourth in the world. . .

JOE BUGNER

And the crowd go wild as they see the shaven head of Hagler enter the auditorium. And there he is, hooded. . .

REG GUTTERIDGE

. . . and **Magri** has to do well against this unknown Mexican who comes from a famous family of five boxing brothers.

HARRY CARPENTER

He's had 24 fights, lost one, so he is undefeated. . .

ALAN MINTER

Born in Italy, most of his fights have been in his native New York.

DESMOND LYNHAM

Minter, the undisputed  world champion, leaves the ring not a champion.

HARRY CARPENTER

Well, I'm hoping we can fight again, or at least have a re-match.

JOHN CONTEH

To be honest, it was a very physical fight. . .

JIM WATT

This ring really does look small although it's standard size. Mind you, we're watching the fight in a huge stadium so Einstein's theory of relativity must be working here.

REG GUTTERIDGE

They've given it all tonight, but there's a little bit left to give yet.

HARRY CARPENTER

# Cricket

It's his second finger — technically his third.
>                   CHRISTOPHER MARTIN-JENKINS

. . . an aggressive back foot drive off the back
foot. . .
>                   TREVOR BAILEY

. . . this series has been swings and pendulums
all the way through.
>                   TREVOR BAILEY

It's a unique occasion, really — a repeat of
Melbourne 1977.
>                   JIM LAKER

It's especially tense for Parker who's literally
fighting for a place on an overcrowded plane
to India.
>                   TREVOR BAILEY

These five weeks have passed at the drop of
a pin.

RACHEL HEYHOE-FLINT


Boycott, somewhat a creature of habit, likes
exactly the sort of food he himself prefers.

DON MOSEY


Now Botham, with a chance to put everything
that's gone before behind him. . .

TONY COSIER


Bill Frindall has done a bit of mental arithmetic
with a calculator. . .

JOHN ARLOTT


The Test Match begins in ten minutes — that's
our time, of course. . .

DAVID COLEMAN


If you're going to lose, you might as well lose
good and proper and try to sneak a win.

TED DEXTER

It is physically and mentally soul-destroying.
GEOFF BOYCOTT

The game's a little bit wide open again.
FRED TRUEMAN

Well, Wally, I've been watching this game both
visually and on TV.
KEN BARRINGTON

He came in from the outfield there like an absolute rabbit.

HENRY BLOFELD

. . . at the end of this match at the Sydney ground the lights have gone out like a flash.

CHRISTOPHER MARTIN-JENKINS

Hardie was a solid rock upon which Essex hung their caps.

PETER WALKER

He's on 90, 10 away from that mythical figure. . .

TREVOR BAILEY

And we have just heard, although this is not the latest score from Bournemouth, that Hampshire have beaten Nottinghamshire by nine wickets.

PETER WEST

Tavare has literally dropped anchor.

TREVOR BAILEY

. . . and Peter Booth, who stands to break a
personal milestone in this match. . .

PETER WALKER

His tail is literally up!

TREVOR BAILEY

Lillee bowled seven overs, no maidens, no wickets for 35, and I think that's a true reflection of his figures, too.

ALAN McGILVRAY

A wicket could always fall in this game, literally at any time.

TREVOR BAILEY

Unless somebody can pull a miracle out of the
fire, Somerset are cruising into the semi-final.
                                    FRED TRUEMAN


. . . and England win by a solitary nine runs. . .
                                    FRANK BOUGH

The obvious successor to Brearley at the
moment isn't obvious.
                                    TREVOR BAILEY

After their 60 overs, West Indies have scored 244 for 7, all out.

FRANK BOUGH

The hallmark of a great captain is the ability to win the toss at the right time.

RICHIE BENAUD

# Cycling

The Tour De France is a totally different ball
game from English cycle-racing.

SIDNEY BENNETT

# Darts

The pendulum swinging back and forth like a
metronome. . .

SID WADDELL

All the psychology of a claymore, Jocky Wilson.
Wilson. . .

SID WADDELL

It [a dart] is almost diametrically in the
middle of the treble twenty.

DAVE LANNING

Tonight, the same as usual, a dartboard with a
difference.

JIM BOWEN

. . . only one word for that — magic darts!

TONY GREEN

Three 140s on the trot — the last one was 100.
SID WADDELL

# Football

Within a couple of minutes he had scored two goals in a two-minute period.
ALAN PARRY

For a player to ask for a transfer has opened everybody's eyebrows.
BOBBY ROBSON

The score is Middlesborough 1, Middlesborough 0 — and Middlesborough have now gone eleven matches without a win.
DAVID COLEMAN

John Bond's smile is always very, very good radio. . .
MIKE INGHAM

Mills is just Mickey Mills and has been Mickey Mills since the year dot.

BOBBY ROBSON


After a goalless first half, the score at half-time is 0-0.

BRIAN MOORE


And Keegan was there like a surgeon's knife — bang!

BRYAN BUTLER


Sporting Lisbon in their green and white hooped shirts. . . they look like a team of zebras.

PETER JONES


So far Villa have only troubled Bradshaw twice with shots that did not trouble him.

LARRY CANNING


Without picking out individuals, I thought Gary Stanley did very well indeed.

ANON

Even when you're dead you shouldn't lie down and let yourself be buried.

GORDON LEE

I'd like to have seen Tony Morley left on as a down and out winger.

JIMMY ARMFIELD

Gary Bailey had to choose tonight to miss out on saving that.

DAVID COLEMAN

And so Tottenham in the last two years have never left London; but now they've been drawn away from home to meet Chelsea.

BRIAN BUTLER

I promise results, not promises.

JOHN BOND

I wouldn't mind being a fly on Larry Lloyd's shorts.

MARTIN JOHNSON

My left foot is not one of my best.

SAMMY McILROY

. . . and their manager, Terry Neil, isn't here
today, which suggests he is elsewhere.

BRIAN MOORE

Most of the things I've done are my own fault,
so I can't feel guilty about them. . .

GEORGE BEST

Football's about 90 minutes on the day; it's about tomorrows really.

GLENN HODDLE

I have other irons in the fire, but I'm keeping them close to my chest.

JOHN BOND

It's been an amazing year for Crystal Palace
over the last 12 months. . .

                    BRIAN MOORE


I don't think they're as good as they are.

                    KEVIN KEEGAN


History, as John Bond would agree, is all about
todays and not about yesterdays.

                    BRIAN MOORE


The advantage of being at home is very much
with the home side.

                    DENIS LAW


Tottenham have got the bullets that can produce
the goods.

                    JIMMY GREAVES


They're still only 1-0 down — if there's such a
thing as only 1-0 down against Brazil.

                    ALAN PARRY

Some of these players never dreamed they'd be playing in a Cup Final at Wembley — but here they are today, fulfilling those dreams.

**LAWRIE McMENEMY**

The Israeli captain has 63 caps under his belt. . .

**DAVID FRANCIE**

Both the Villa scorers, Withe and Mortimer, were born in Liverpool — as was the Villa manager Ron Saunders, who was born in Birkenhead.

DAVID COLEMAN

Aston Villa began to harness the fruits of some good midfield work.

ALAN TOWERS

. . . so different from the scenes in 1872, at the Cup Final that none of us can remember.

JOHN MOTSON


. . . and now, the familiar sight of Liverpool raising the League Cup for the first time.

BRIAN MOORE


They [Coventry City FC] can beat anybody on the day, but they can also lose against anybody on the day.

EMLYN HUGHES


That one sold Wilkins a lot of trouble, giving Mortimer an easy bite of the ball.

HUGH JOHNS


Four-nil up, they [Bristol Rovers] were at half-time − all in the first half, those.

TONY ADAMSON


With the very last kick of the game, Bobby McDonald scored with a header.

ALAN PARRY

Brooking trying one of those impossible crosses, which on that occasion was impossible. . .

BRIAN MOORE


Queens Park against Forfar — you can't get more romantic than that.

ARCHIE McPHERSON


Nick Holmes also got two today, as Southampton won 3-0 at Leeds. Nick Holmes got the other.

TONY GUBBA


Last time Brighton and Manchester United met they drew two-all, and two of these were Manchester United's.

DAVID COLEMAN


Harlow are in their infancy compared to other giant-killing giants.

PETER LORENZO

He [Graham Rix] was not so much off-colour
as not quite on song yesterday.

JIMMY HILL

If we can stop hooliganism, we can go a long
way towards stemming this great tide of people
not going to football matches.

BRIAN CLOUGH

If there wasn't such a thing as football, we'd all be frustrated footballers.

MICK LYONS

He's got three goals in four games — you can't beat that.

STUART HALL

Exeter 3, Swindon 4 — a good tight defensive game there.

BRIAN BUTLER

. . . and Southampton have beaten Brighton by three goals to one; that's a repeat of last year's result, when Southampton won 5-1.

DESMOND LINEHAM

West Ham. . . like actors playing to an empty stage.

BRIAN BUTLER

I don't think, Brian. You don't think in this game.

ALLAN CLARKE

Liverpool always seem to find a boot at the right moment to keep Birmingham City at arm's length.

CLIVE TILSLEY

All the team are 100% behind the manager, but I can't speak for the rest of the squad.

BRIAN GREENHOFF

In fact, I'll stick my neck out and say that whichever side wins this match might win the Cup.

FRED TRUEMAN

You can imagine how they feel. . . surrounded
by their manager Ron Greenwood.

DICKIE DAVIES

We don't always get from slow motion the
pace at which they play.

JOHN BARRETT

When it's all said and done, that's the moment when the talking has to stop.

JIMMY HILL

And Ritchie has now scored 11 goals, exactly double the number he scored last season.

ALAN PARRY

Well, it's Ipswich 0, Liverpool 2, and if that's the way the score stays then you've got to fancy Liverpool to win.

PETER JONES

He's got a left foot, and left foots are like bricks of gold.

JIMMY GREAVES

Thank you for evoking memories — particularly of days gone by.

MIKE INGHAM

You can't really call yourselves giant-killers any more, as you kill giants so often.

BRIAN BUTLER

So Liverpool are ahead two-one. It couldn't be a closer lead.

PETER JONES

I'm sure that when Kevin Keegan arrives at the Dell, the fans will give him a great send-off.

ALAN BALL

Lawrenson slipped the ball through to Williams, and he beat Shilton from 35 yards. . . and you don't beat Shilton from 35 yards.

PETER JONES

What a goal from Trevor Francis. That was
$1,000,000, let alone £1,000,000.

BRIAN BUTLER


There aren't many last chances left for him
[George Best].

ARCHIE MacPHERSON


Kilmarnock versus Partick Thistle, match post-
poned. . . that, of course, is a latest score.

FRANK BOUGH


That chance was too easy. If it had been harder
he probably would have scored.

DENIS LAW


It was Forest's night on Tuesday, but it looks
like being Liverpool's night this afternoon.

PETER JONES


The goal must have looked completely
enormous for Dalglish then.

DAVID COLEMAN

I would advise anyone coming to the match to come early and not leave until the end, otherwise they might miss something.

JOHN TOSHACK

2-0 is a fair reflection of the scoreline.

GEOFF HURST

. . . saved by Bailey, son of Roy Bailey, once the Ipswich goalkeeper. He's no longer being called the son of Roy Bailey.

PETER JONES

Pat Jennings clapped his hand round the ball like banging a piece of toast.

BARRY DAVIS

There's Kevin Reeves, who's just turned 22, and proving an ill wind blows nobody any good.

DAVID COLEMAN

Bolton are on the crest of a slump.

ANON

Ayr 1, Arbroath 0 — Arbroath still without an away win of any kind.

DAVID COLEMAN

You couldn't have counted the number of moves Alan Ball made. . . I counted four and possibly five.

JOHN MOTSON

My father was a miner and he worked down a mine.

KEVIN KEEGAN

You could cut the atmosphere with a knife, it was so electric.

BRIAN MARJORIBANKS

... Hollins, of course, never believes that a match has finished until the final whistle has blown.

PETER JONES

He hit that one like an arrow.

ALAN PARRY


Peter Ward has become a new man. Just like his old self.

JIM ROSENTHAL


The Bulgarians are going forward, more in hope than optimism.

PETER JONES


There's nothing like second best, and that's what Liverpool are not!

JIM ROSENTHAL


. . . the European Cup, almost 17 pounds of silver that's worth its weight in gold.

BRIAN MOORE


Well, the game isn't over yet, there's still 83 minutes to go.

SWISS TV COMMENTATOR

That was Borissov. . . the man with the left foot.
JOHN MOTSON

Dalglish — he's the sort of player who's so unique.
BOB WILSON

Bulgaria were quite literally not at the match.
GEORGE HAMILTON


. . . the ball has broken 50/50 for Kevin Keegan.
DAVID COLEMAN

Well, gentlemen, when one team scores early in the game it often takes an early lead.

PAT MARSDEN

We are now into the third and final quarter of this game.

IRISH TV COMMENTATOR

And there'll be more football in a moment, but first we've got the highlights of the Scottish League Cup Final.

GARY NEWBON

Norwich's goal was scored by Kevin Bond, who is the son of his father.

FRANK BOUGH

# Golf

And, on the eve of the Bob Hope Classic. . . an interview with the man himself, Gerry Ford.

JIM ROSENTHAL

You couldn't really find two more completely
different personalities than these two men, Tom
Watson and Brian Barnes; one the complete golf
professional and the other the complete professional golfer.

PETER ALLISS

PETER ALLISS: What do you think of the
climax of this tournament?
PETER THOMSON: I'm speechless.
PETER ALLISS: That says it all.

# Horses

It looks as though that premature excitement
may have been premature.

BROUGH SCOTT

And Harvey Smith is on the phone now and I
think that means he's on the phone.

RAYMOND BROOKES-WARD

. . . and there's the unmistakable figure of Joe
Mercer. . . or is it Lester Piggott?

**BROUGH SCOTT**

That's the magic of television – I've just heard
over the headphones that Noalto was third.

**DAVID COLEMAN**

So far this year there haven't been any world-class steeplechase times anywhere in the world.

**DAVID COLEMAN**

# Ice Skating

Robin Cousins, with a superficial face wound on his leg.

**NICKY STEELE**

# Motor Sport

You can cut the tension with a cricket stump.

MURRAY WALKER

He's in front of everyone in this race except for the two in front of him. . .

MURRAY WALKER

. . . into lap 53, the penultimate last lap but one. . .

MURRAY WALKER

Alan Jones has carved the gap down from ten seconds to two. . .

MURRAY WALKER

Here's Giacomelli — driving like the veteran he is not.

MURRAY WALKER

There's enough Ferraris there to eat a plate of spaghetti.

JACKIE STEWART

. . . only ten of the starters who began this race are left.

MURRAY WALKER

I make no apologies for their absence; I'm sorry they're not here. . .

MURRAY WALKER

The battle is well and truly on if it wasn't on before, and it certainly was.

MURRAY WALKER

# Oddballs

. . . and how long have you had this lifelong ambition?

GARY DAVIS

The speed of light is very fast.

CARL SAGAN

Tell me what you do for a living — you're an insurance broker, aren't you?

EAMONN ANDREWS

Two million pounds' worth of priceless prints and drawings have already been moved there. . .

DR ROY STRONG

Conditions on the road are bad, so if you are just setting off for work, leave a little earlier.

**KELVIN O'SHEA**

For people who like that sort of thing, that's the sort of thing they like.

**JOE JACKSON**

And today we have in the studio an optician,
who will answer any questions you may or may
not have about reading glasses.

TONY GILMAN


Absolutely right. You're walking through this
competition like a piece of cake.

MIKE READ


He's bitten off a bit more than he can chew.

BROTHER OF HUNGER-STRIKER
RAYMOND McCREESH


. . . and now for a blow-by-blow account of the
shooting. . .

PETER SISSONS


It's a mixed bag of economic indicators but
there are straws in the wind.

MICHAEL GREEN


Back home, A.J. Cronin, creator of Dr Finlay's
Casebook, has died in Switzerland. . .

PETER SISSONS

. . . and now to the subjects of law, and inter-national law — subjects usually as dry as ditch-water.

JOAN BAKEWELL

I must apologise to the deaf for the loss of subtitles.

ANGELA RIPPON

. . . and at 10.30pm 'Farewell My Lovely', with Robert Mitchum in the title role. . .
**ATV PRESENTER**

It's so true to life it's hardly true.
**MICHAEL ASPEL**

Once again the last-minute bogey has struck.
**PETER SLATER**

Some of the crowd have decided to voice their opinion by staying away.
**DOUGIE DONNELLY**

So the VAT increase on a secondhand car is just another added addition.
**ADRIAN LOVE**

In first place there is an absolute dead-heat tie.
**MAGNUS MAGNUSSON**

The dispute went on escalating like a snowball.
**WILLIAM DEEDES**

. . . and for those of you watching who haven't television sets, live commentary is on Radio 2.

DAVID COLEMAN


. . . and the booze will be flowing like wine in Arbroath today.

SIMON BATES


We're ten years old this week. It's a one-off thing. It won't happen again for another ten years.

BOB ELLIOTT


. . . it's like feeding him with one hand and spitting at him in the eye with the other.

CLARE RAYNER


Send in your competition answers with your name, age, and how old you are.

TONY BLACKBURN


Gilmore could have lived for as long as he liked. He could have lived for the rest of his life.

NORMAN MAILER

A fast has no real nutritional value.

'A DIETICIAN'


I have already not made that point.

DAVID FROST


Sir Anthony Blunt is the acknowledged
authority on the French painter Nicholas
Poisson (sic).

CHRIS UNDERWOOD


If Tchaikovsky was alive today he'd be turning
in his grave.

SIMON BOOKER


Quarante-deux secondes. . . that's about forty-
two seconds.

STUART HALL


Our walking encyclopaedia on disablement
problems, Ann Davies, is waiting in her wheel-
chair to hear from you.

ROBBIE VINCENT

The robbery was committed by a pair of identical twins. Both are said to be aged about 20.

PAUL HOLLINGSWORTH


We apologise for the late running of this train. This is due to us following a train that is in front of us.

BRITISH RAIL GUARD


Well, we seem to have had a morning of Bach and Mozart, like that last piece by Tchaikovsky.

HONG KONG RADIO ANNOUNCER


53 points – a world record. I don't think that's been equalled before.

STUART HALL


You don't get once-in-a-lifetime offers like this every day...

ADVERTISEMENT


... fifty-eight per cent of all cars coming into Britain are imported...

MONTY MODLYN

. . . Channel Tunnel project which seems to be getting off the ground again.

JAMES LONG

Most gays have heterosexual parents. . .

ANONYMOUS GAY PERSON

Women are the greatest heroines of the sagas.
MAGNUS MAGNUSSON

Ah yes, Mohammed — that's one of the most common Christian names in the world.
KID JENSEN

At 7. . . Eamonn will approach another surprised personality with his famous three words — 'This Is Your Life'.
KATHY SECKER

If you let nettles grow near your raspberry canes they'll shoot up like ninepins.
GARDENERS' QUESTION TIME

This is an age-old controversy that has been going on for the last 20 years.
LAWRIE QUAYLE

Women are finding a much more vocal voice in the theatre.
JANE LAPOTAIRE

After a period of years the new skin gets older and older.

DR ALAN MARION-DAVIS

Stronsay is an island surrounded by sea.

FIONA JOHNSTON

I like to sit in the shade of a tree and soak up the sun.

JOE GORMLEY

We'll be back at the same time next week at the slightly later time of ten past eleven.

MICHAEL DORAN

The good thing about these dark evenings is that you can't see how dark and horrible it is outside.

TONY BLACKBURN

We all thought this book 'Joseph' was incredible — very convincing.

LORD BRIGGS

Some news has just come in — it's so hot the paper's still wet.

ANDY PEEBLES


We all have some sort of chip on our shoulder which we want to get off our chest. . .

KERRY JUBY


He lived until he was 80 — from when he was born until he died.

HUNTER DAVIES


In one consecutive hour we had two programmes on the same subject.

DEREK JAMESON


Traffic in the Wandsworth one-way system is very heavy in both directions.

GRAHAM DENE


I feel we are the only country in the world that doesn't have a British film industry any more.

JOAN COLLINS

We have something fiendish planned but enough
of that later.

STUART HALL

One saw the face of British humour being
changed single-handedly . . . almost by one man.

MICHAEL YORK

He [Ned Sherrin] contributed more to television
in the 1950s and '60s than anyone before or
since.

ARIANNA STASSINOPOULOS

There they are, every colour of the rainbow:
black, white, brown. . .

ANON

It's four minutes to eight — that's the time.

GRAHAM DENE

. . . and I think Valentino would have suffered
the same death had he lived.

KING VIDOR

Agatha Christie is such a well-known name, her books sell all over the world — and other places as well.

MICHAEL GRADE

It's one of those things you wouldn't know unless you knew it.

DAVE JAMIESON

This week's mailbag topic is 'Is Christianity Eyewash?' — which is quite a statement.

ANDY PEEBLES

This great Elizabethan house, dating back to the reign of Elizabeth. . .

DORIAN WILLIAMS

There's a paratrooper coming down now. Let's see if he's going to land. . .

TONY BLACKBURN

Aircraft are central to Western Air Policy.

MICHAEL RAMSDEN

Here comes the conductor of Mozart's
Symphony No 29 in A-Major. . . by Mozart.

**RICHARD BAKER**

. . . that programme was so interesting. . . I
learnt things I never even knew. . .

**ADRIAN LOVE**

John Wayne — a man literally larger than life!
It's hard to believe that he's no longer with us.

**STEVE JONES**

At the moment we're testing the performance
of the engine on this engine performance tester.

**BERNARD CLARK**

It was a sudden and unexpected surprise.

**OLD BAILEY CORRESPONDENT, BBC**

What will radio programmes be like in a hundred
years' time? Let's go forward to the year 2000
and find out!

**PAUL BURNETT**

We are literally giving away Zeta One movie cameras together with a money-back guarantee.

EMPEROR ROSKO

There's a sight to take your breath away — the smell of hyacinths.

PETER SEABROOK

# Politics

The crunch has been reached. The crying wolves are out the window.

ALEX KITSON

[Denis Healey is] not looking like a man who's had a tremendous victory, which indeed he hasn't.

DAVID DIMBLEBY

I'm hopeful until the last hour of the last minute.

ALEX KITSON

We are not prepared to stand idly by and be
murdered in our beds.

REV IAN PAISLEY

The Fermanagh by-election is not about the IRA
hunger strikes, but about bread and butter issues.

EAMONN MALLEY

The government is clutching at sport as a straw
with which to beat the Russians.

PETER LAWSON

... but yesterday Sir Peter [Parker] played the
final card in what's been a tricky game of chess.

**JOHN PERKINS**

The Conservatives' policy of non-intervention
to support ailing industry is a hot potato which
could leave the Government with egg all over its
face.

**NEWS COMMENTATOR**

... the Unionist Parliament was without spine
or backbone.

**REV IAN PAISLEY**

Fighting broke out in the Indian Parliament and one 'Untouchable' MP was punched on the nose.
BBC RADIO FOUR NEWS


Mrs Thatcher. . . greeted by a small multitude.
MICHAEL CHARLTON


In the case of my own case, this has not been the case.
PETER TATCHELL

# Pop

The Police, down one place to number two —
they just didn't make it to number one.
                                        TONY BLACKBURN


That one sounds as if it was made in 1965 but
in fact it's older than that — it came out in
1972. . .
                                        MIKE SMITH


Welcome to our lunchtime soiree. . .
                                        NICKY HORNE


It got to the stage that you could hardly open a
tabloid without seeing them [John Lennon and
Yoko Ono] on the front cover. . .
                                        NEWSBEAT


I visited Bob Marley's grave. It was on an in-
accessible mountain top.
                                        'WEEKENDING'

. . . another example of a record company
soaking an album till it's dry.

> PETER POWELL

. . . at 9.00 this evening we will broadcast 10
minutes of silence. . .

> GEOFF BENSON

It has often been said that George Harrison was
the fifth Beatle. . .

> CAPITAL RADIO DJ

. . . and now a word from George Harrison, who
was said to have known John Lennon very well.

> CAPITAL RADIO NEWSCASTER

They've written their own number — it's an
original number and it's written by themselves.

> JENNY LEE-WRIGHT

. . . great record there from America, that great
three-piece trio.

> ANDY PEEBLES

The runner-up in second place is Linda Lewis.

TONY MONOPOLY

Helen Reddy — the acceptable face of middle-of-the-road.

NICKY HORNE

It's surprising — all the Beatles are still older than the Shadows, after all this time!

NICK LOWE

. . . that Errol Garner style — inimitable style — which has been imitated by more pianists than you've had hot dinners.

HUMPHREY LYTTLETON

And at number five, down seven places, the Gibson Brothers. . .

KID JENSEN

This is another man who has influenced me more than anybody else: John Lennon.

JIMMY PURSEY

The record of Buddy Holly I like best is one he made before he died.

DAVID HEPWORTH

. . . a lot of new albums out that we'll be hearing quite a lot of, because they sound like albums that will remain timeless for quite some time.

KID JENSEN

He was one of the all-time greats of all time.

FEE WAYBILL

. . . and thanks too for the signed autograph.

TONY BLACKBURN

It's so easy to have a fatal accident and ruin your life.

TONY BLACKBURN

Marc Bolan and T. Rex there — sounding as good as the day he recorded it.

TOMMY VANCE

I don't know where Jefferson Starship are. . . I lost track of what they were doing recently a long time ago.

ANNE NIGHTINGALE

'She Moves Through the Fair' is a very old song . . . and . . . continues to be old.

MARGARET BARRY

That was Bob Dylan, who was, and still is, white.

DEREK JEWELL

. . . and a massive leap for Liquid Gold of one place to number four. . .

TONY BLACKBURN

# Royalty

Even to my untrained eye it looks as though she has a long train. . .

RONALD ALLISON

The luggage has already departed — that's why we're all so excited.

TOM FLEMING

And for those of you who don't know Australia House, it's a beautiful Victorian building. . . the first brick was laid in 1913 by King George V.

ROLF HARRIS

. . . they're waving their flags ten to the dozen.

LORRAINE CHASE

. . . not only is it the start of their honeymoon,
it's the start of their married life together.

ANGELA RIPPON

. . . and some of the fireworks will go whizz-
bang, and some will go bang-whizz.

ALASTAIR BURNETT

# Rugby

... and if they can get some pressure going, they'll put them under pressure...

GARETH EDWARDS

It could be a broken wrist — or, at the worst, a very bad sprain.

JOHN BOYD

... so near and yet so close came the Irish to success...

IRISH RADIO COMMENTATOR

Of course, the Australian people here are over-joyed because that puts England ahead.

BILL McLAREN

... this will put the pressure back on Great Britain, which they can ill-afford to do without.

ALEX MURPHY

Rafter, again doing much of the unseen work
which the crowd relishes so much. . .

BILL McLAREN


And let's see where that move started. And it
started from its origins. . .

EDDIE WARING


. . . and Dusty Hare kicked 19 of the 17 points.

DAVID COLEMAN


There's one minute sixty seconds to go. . .

EDDIE WARING

# Snooker

Hurricane Higgins can either win or lose this
final match tomorrow. . .

ARCHIE McPHERSON

It's not easy to get a snooker when there's only
one ball on the table.

TED LOWE

A two frame lead is really only one.

EDDIE CHARLTON

He made a break of 98 which was almost one hundred.

ALAN WEEKS

This of course is a shot that Ray's an expert at ... that's seven points away.

TED LOWE

The table that they're playing on is in fact the pride and property of the late and great Joe Davis.

TED LOWE

It's at times like these that you have to clench your teeth together and say a prayer.

TED LOWE

This has been the story of his life for most of this match.

CLIVE EVERTON

When he [Alex 'Hurricane' Higgins] has got his tail up, he's a very hard nut to crack.

JACK KARNHAM

And that's the third time he's done that this
session. He's missed his waistcoat pocket with
the chalk.

TED LOWE

Perrie Mans played a prominent part in this
tournament in 1979 — in fact he won it. . .

TED LOWE

One mistake here could win or lose the match either way.

TED LOWE

And Alex has literally come back from the dead!
TED LOWE

Cliff [Thorburn] has been unsettled by the erratic but consistent potting of Perrie Mans.

TED LOWE

We've had three other snooker centuries. . . this will make the fifth.

TED LOWE

It's always nice to get the first frame under your belt. It means your opponent has to get two frames to gain the lead.

JOHN PULMAN

The audience are literally electrified and glued to their seats.

TED LOWE

Although he's virtually won this match now he still really needs to win it.

JOHN PULMAN

I am speaking from a deserted and virtually empty Crucible Theatre.

DAVID VINE

Griffiths is snookered on the brown, which, for those of you watching in black and white, is the ball directly behind the pink.

TED LOWE

# Tennis

That's John McEnroe in a familiar pose, doing something to his shoelaces that never seem to be the way they want him to be.

JOHN BARRETT

Seeds started to tumble like flies being knocked off a wall.

DAVID VINE

Now is the time for both players to sit back and relax, take their minds right off the game and think what tactics to employ in the next set.

ANNE JONES

Nobody has worked harder than Gottfried to get to the top of the tennis tree, and certainly nobody more so than Borg.

DAN MASKELL

This is a sheer game of chess between these two players. But Borg has an ace in the pack.

MAX ROBERTSON

. . . a sudden burst of consistency from Feaver. . .

DAN MASKELL

So many ambitions lie buried on the surface of these famous clay courts.

GERALD WILLIAMS

Miss Ruzici was absolutely committed to going one way or the other.

BILL THRELFALL

Roscoe Tanner is one of the great runners-up of all time. No man could have played better.

DAN MASKELL

Well, of its kind it's gripping tennis because nobody knows the outcome.

PETER WEST


Oh! That cross-court angle was so acute it doesn't exist.

DAN MASKELL


It looks as though the end is over.

DAN MASKELL


CARPENTER: Do you think Tanner has a real chance of beating Borg today?
MASKELL: Not a real chance, but he has a chance.


Miss Stove seems to be going off the boil.

PETER WEST


. . . the almost immortal Billy Jean. . .

HARRY CARPENTER

Here is Tanner ready to serve — with a curly haircut this year. Must be a lucky omen for him: first time with a curly haircut and first time in a Wimbledon final.

**JOHN MOTSON**

You can read

**Colemanballs**

every issue
in

# PRIVATE EYE